Called to Serve, Called to Lead

Reflections on the Ministerial Priesthood
by Archbishop Joseph L. Bernardin

Cover and book design by Julie Van Leeuwen.

SBN 0-912228-94-6

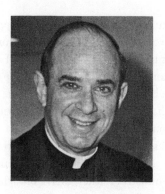

My dear brothers in Christ:

 THE fifteenth anniversary of
my episcopal ordination has given me an opportunity I
have long sought: to share with my fellow priests of the
Presbyterium of Cincinnati some thoughts and convictions
about the life and ministry to which the Lord has called us
through the Sacrament of Holy Orders. In the eight years I
have had the privilege of serving as bishop for the Church
of Cincinnati, I have come to know my brother priests
well. Together we have grown during this time: in priestly
affection for one another and in respect for the many gifts
with which the Lord has blessed us.

Fortunately, we have had many opportunities to pray together and discuss our common vision of priestly ministry, our hopes and aspirations, as well as our frustrations and difficulties. Our friendship and collaboration have been precious gifts to me. From this relationship have come many of the reflections I want to share with you at this time.

In this pastoral letter I have not attempted a complete theological review of the ministerial priesthood and priestly ministry. Rather, I have brought together some ideas I have expressed over the past years before various groups and in private conversations. In particular, I have incorporated the substance of a day of recollection on priestly spirituality I gave recently to the priests of the Archdiocese.

I hope that this letter will serve as a basis for further reflection and dialogue among all priests. It is for this reason that I share these thoughts with those outside the Archdiocese of Cincinnati. If this letter helps to deepen your understanding and appreciation of the priesthood, then my effort will have been worthwhile.

Contents

Our Priestly Identity   1

Our Priestly Ministry   9

Personal Qualities for Effective Ministry   25

The Prayer Life of the Priest   33

Afterword   52

Our Priestly Identity

THERE is only one
priesthood, the priesthood of Jesus Christ. Jesus is the sole
mediator between the human family and God. He has
redeemed us by appearing "at the end of all ages to take
away sins once for all by his sacrifice." (Heb. 9:26) We
participate in this priesthood in different ways.

There is the priesthood of all believers, shared by
all the baptized, laity and clergy alike. The First Letter of
Peter, thought by scripture scholars to be a baptismal
homily, tells the candidates for baptism: "You, however,
are a chosen race, a royal priesthood, a holy nation, a

people he claims for his own to proclaim the glorious works of the One who called you from darkness into his marvelous light." (1 Pet. 2:9) "Come to him, a living stone, rejected by men but approved, nonetheless, and precious in God's eyes," Peter tells these new Christians. "You too are living stones, built as an edifice of spirit, into a holy priesthood, offering spiritual sacrifices acceptable to God through Jesus Christ . . . . As generous distributors of God's manifold grace, put your gifts at the service of one another, each in the measure he has received." (1 Pet. 2:4-5 and 4:10) We exercise this priesthood of all believers by offering God lives sanctified by doing everything for love of Him and one another. Christians are indeed priests of their own lives.

There is also the ordained or ministerial priesthood, a ministry of word, of sacrament, and of charity. This priesthood, which has certain resemblances to the Levitical priesthood of the Old Testament, centers on the Eucharist. Although it is unique and indispensable, willed by Christ, it does not supplant the priesthood of all believers but complements it. As the Second Vatican Council has stated: "Though they differ from one another in essence and not only in degree, the common priesthood of the faithful and the ministerial or hierarchical priesthood are nonetheless interrelated. Each of them in its own special way is a participation in the one priesthood of Christ."[1]

According to our Catholic tradition, Holy Orders is a sacrament shared by bishops, presbyters, and deacons. The bishop enjoys the fullness of the ministerial priesthood. Presbyters and deacons participate with him in this sacrament in different degrees. Together the three orders reflect the full richness of the sacrament and the essential unity of its ministry, which is basically a ministry not of domination but of service to God's people.

Pope John Paul II, in his many reflections on the ministerial priesthood, has stressed the importance of maintaining our priestly *identity*. He has also spoken about the danger of secularizing the priesthood. Some have felt uncomfortable with this counsel, fearing it meant that priests should withdraw from the world or not become involved in the daily joys and sorrows of the human condition. This is certainly not the Holy Father's message.

Several years ago, the Lutheran theologian Jaroslav Pelikan summed up the inner nature and mission of the Church in two words: identity and universality. "By identity," he said, "I mean that which distinguishes the Church from the world — its message, its uniqueness, its particularity. By universality, on the other hand, I mean that which impels the Church to embrace nothing less than all mankind in its vision and its appeal."[2] There will always be a tension between the Church's identity and its universality. Resolving this tension by neglecting one at the expense of the other would involve unfaithfulness to the Church's Lord. If we go too far in the direction of universality, we lose our identity as a community of believers; our specific vision of life and our mission becomes blurred. Exclusive emphasis on our identity, on the other hand, turns the Church into a sect: spiritually pure, perhaps, but increasingly irrelevant and unfruitful for those outside.

I believe Pelikan's insight into the Church's identity and universality throws light on the Holy Father's emphasis on *priestly* identity. The egalitarian spirit of our times prompts us to downplay differences in roles and responsibilities. It is good to be reminded of the need to maintain constructive tension between identity and universality. This tension is certainly implicit in what Isaiah said of the Servant of the Lord: "The Spirit of the Lord God is upon me, because the Lord has anointed me; he has sent me to bring glad tidings to the lowly, to heal the brokenhearted, to proclaim liberty to the captives and release to the prisoners." (Isaiah, 61:1)

The Servant had a *universal* call. He was sent to minister to *all* people: not just "nice" people who had made their way in the world but also, and indeed especially, the poor and the outcast, those who were down and out, who had little to look forward to. Yet the Servant also had a special identity. He was the Lord's *anointed.* In the Old Testament, anointing with richly fragrant oils signified dedication to God for a special purpose. Humanly speaking, Isaiah's Servant was no different from anyone else. But because of God's special election, of which his anointing was the outward sign, the Servant's words had special meaning and authority, and his actions were done in power. Jesus consciously assumed this identity when He presented Himself to His people in the synagogue at Nazareth. When He read this familiar passage from Isaiah on that occasion, Jesus was claiming for Himself the title of Messiah, the anointed one *par excellence.* (Cf.Luke, 4:16-20)

It is in Jesus, whose priesthood we share, that we discover our own specific identity as priests of the New Covenant. Like Jesus, we are chosen, anointed, and sent forth to proclaim the good news of salvation in the kingdom which He announced. Our calling and anointing, which enable us to share in a special way in the power of God's Spirit, give us our identity as priests. We are instruments who minister "in the person of Christ."[3] We have a unique role in the Church because we are called to be "an effective sign and witness to the Church's faith in the reconciling Christ, who works through the Church and through the one whom the Church has sent to be the steward of its gifts and services."[4] This special identity, however, does not make us better than others, nor does it entitle us to special privileges. But it does signify who we are, whom we represent, what our mission is, and what demands are made of us in regard to spiritual growth and commitment to others.

Moreover, this priestly identity is not superficial or something we can hide or discard. It is not a part-time reality. No matter where we are, what we are doing, whom we are serving, we are "marked" men who must openly give witness to the special mission Christ has shared with us. To try to hide or downplay this special calling — this divine election — by espousing values or adopting a life style contrary to those evident in the life and ministry of Jesus, would be to cloud our true identity and ultimately to betray our vocation.

To understand and appreciate our priesthood, we must turn to Jesus. From Him alone we can obtain wisdom, guidance, and strength to fashion our priestly ministry and live up to our priestly commitment. Any attempt to explain the priesthood apart from the mystery of Christ and His Church is fruitless. Any attempt to tear the ministerial priesthood from its roots in Christ and the Church will bring disillusionment and failure. It is precisely the effort, however unconscious or even well-intentioned, to explain priesthood in purely human terms, to rob it of its essentially spiritual task of bringing people the reconciliation with the Father accomplished by Christ, that has caused confusion and pain among the best of us. Speaking to the priests of Rome in November, 1978, the Holy Father said: "Let us not deceive ourselves that we are serving the Gospel if we try to 'water down' our priestly charism through exaggerated interest in the vast field of temporal problems, if we wish to 'secularize' our way of living and acting, if we cancel even the external signs of our priestly vocation."[5] No more than the men and women of St. Paul's day can we conform ourselves to the present age and still remain true to our vocation. (Cf. Rom. 12:2)

Our Priestly Ministry

IN the exhortation of the
Roman Pontifical, the man to be ordained is told that he is
"to serve Christ the Teacher, Priest and Shepherd in his
ministry which is to make his own body, the Church, grow
into the people of God, a holy temple." The Pontifical then
goes on to say that "by consecration he will be made a true
priest of the New Testament, to preach the Gospel, sustain
God's people, and celebrate the liturgy, above all, the
Lord's sacrifice."[6] Let us consider each of these three
charges.

We Are Teachers

Paul's rhetorical questions in the tenth chapter of his letter to the Romans have lost none of their force. " 'Everyone who calls on the name of the Lord will be saved.' But how shall they call on him in whom they have not believed? And how can they believe unless they have heard of him? And how can they hear unless there is someone to preach? And how can men preach unless they are sent?" (Rom. 10:13-15) We receive that commission in ordination. Teaching ministry is essential to the ministerial priesthood.

An authentic prophet or teacher preaches God's message, not his own. God made this clear when He commissioned Jeremiah. "Whatever I command you, you shall speak . . . See, I place my words in your mouth!" (Jer. 1:7-9) Paul had the same understanding of his calling. "It is not ourselves we preach," he told the Corinthians, "but Christ Jesus as Lord." (2 Cor. 4:5)

As ministers of the word, we too must remember that it is the Lord's gospel we preach, not our own. Certainly we must use all our talents to present the message entrusted to us in the most creative, compelling manner possible. But in doing so, we must be careful not to distort this message in any way. Above all, we must not place obstacles in the way of its saving power by projecting our own ideas and prejudices. This requires intellectual honesty and humility. It also demands fidelity to the teaching authority of the Church, which has from Christ the responsibility of handing on His message in all its richness and without error. Moreover, it requires that we internalize God's word ourselves. Otherwise our teaching will lack credibility.

Preaching the gospel in its full integrity is not always easy. The gospel challenges people's complacency; frequently it upsets their consciences; it unnerves them by demanding that they change their way of life. In consequence they may try to discredit the gospel's teaching by attacking the teacher. Jeremiah understood this all too well and tried to use his youth as an excuse to evade his calling. But God told him not to worry: "Have no fear, because I am with you to deliver you." (Jer. 1:8) Paul also understood the hazard of preaching the gospel, but, knowing that God would help him, he never hesitated to carry out his task. "I am content," he told the Corinthians, "with weakness, with mistreatment, with distress, with persecutions and difficulties for the sake of Christ; for when I am powerless, it is then that I am strong." (2 Cor. 12:10)

As teachers of the word, we too must always place ourselves completely in the hands of the Lord, convinced that as long as we do our part He will never fail us. It is that abandonment which gives us strength and makes our message not only believable but exciting.

Today we face a particular difficulty: People generally no longer accept at face value the pronouncements of institutions or the rationales which they give for their policies or programs. They have become much more independent in their thinking. They want reasons for adopting a position, and they reserve the right to decide for themselves whether or not they will accept the reasons and embrace the position.

This naturally affects the way people receive the Church's teaching. We believe the authorized teachers of the Church — that is, the Holy Father and the bishops in union with him — receive special guidance from the Holy Spirit so that God's message will never be betrayed or falsified. Today, however, much of the Church's teaching is challenged and even contradicted. This is especially true in regard to morality. The Church's teaching concerning human sexuality, marriage, and social justice, for example, simply does not have the impact it should on many people. Many look on moral teaching as a laundry list of do's and don'ts, based more on historical accident or institutional concern than a gospel mandate. So they pick and choose what they want and reject the rest.

This new situation challenges us to develop a fresh approach, without authoritarianism on the one hand or a take-it-or-leave-it spirit on the other. We need a greater evangelistic effort. The intellectual dimension should not be minimized, and well-reasoned arguments in support of faith are essential. But they are not enough. Before people can fully live by the values Jesus taught, they must experience *conversion.* They must come to know and love the Lord. They must experience Him in their lives; His love, mercy, understanding, and compassion must be real to them. Only then will they be willing to commit themselves to Him and accept the demands He makes. Only then will they be ready to make the surrender expected of every Christian.

People who experience conversion begin to understand that they are called to a totally new way of life, one involving new personal and societal responsibilities and running counter to many values of contemporary culture. Such people find that the demands of the gospel, which humanly speaking may seem impossible, are not only possible but can even be accepted willingly and joyfully in consequence of God's grace and the strength which it confers. Even when they are weak and do not live up to the Lord's expectations, they do not despair. They ask for forgiveness and begin again.

The call to conversion is universal. From the very beginning of His public ministry Jesus' constant theme was: "Reform your lives! The kingdom of heaven is at hand." (Matt. 4:17) Conversion is critically important for us as priests. "If we have the duty of helping others to be converted," Pope John Paul II said, "we have to do the same continuously in our lives."[7] Pope Paul VI reminded us that unless our lives reflect simplicity, prayerfulness, justice and charity toward all — especially the lowly and the poor — obedience and humility, detachment and self-sacrifice, "our word will have difficulty in touching the heart of modern man. It risks being vain and sterile."[8]

In the context of our living, personal relationship with Christ, His teaching takes on a deeper and richer meaning. Learning about His message becomes an exciting adventure when one realizes that fidelity to Christ's teaching is an important measure of personal fidelity to Him, while infidelity or indifference to what He teaches calls into question the authenticity of one's commitment to Him.

We Are Leaders of the Worshipping Community

As ordained ministers, we share in Christ's sanctifying power through the celebration of the sacraments which are real encounters with the Lord. In a special way, we are called to be ministers of the Eucharist. In his 1980 Letter on the Mystery and Worship of the Holy Eucharist, the Holy Father said: "The Eucharist is the principal and central raison d'être of the Sacrament of the priesthood, which effectively came into being at the moment of the institution of the Eucharist, and together with it. Through our ordination . . . we are united in a singular and exceptional way to the Eucharist. In a certain way we derive *from* it and exist *for* it."[9]

Understood in this way, the Eucharist provides the foundation, the vision, and the dynamism for our entire priestly ministry. It is in the Eucharist that we encounter Jesus. We encounter Him in His word which is proclaimed. We encounter Him as our Savior who gave Himself for us in the sacrifice on the cross. We encounter Him as the Bread of Life. This Eucharistic encounter with the Lord, which enables us to share with Him the wonders of the paschal mystery, is necessary for the spiritual well-being of all the faithful. But it gives special meaning and direction to our lives and ministry as priests.

The Eucharist, if permitted to have its full effect, will never allow us to stand still, to grow complacent toward ourselves or others. The Eucharist, as Pope John Paul II said, causes us to know ourselves better because it perfects "the image of God that we bear within ourselves."[10] It also helps us grow in our awareness of the dignity of others, an awareness, the Holy Father said, which "becomes the deepest motive of our relationship with our neighbor."[11] For this reason the Second Vatican Council rightly said that the Liturgy, in particular the Eucharist, is the "summit toward which the activity of the Church is directed; it is also the fount from which all her power flows."[12]

A frequently quoted passage from the Letter to the Hebrews, describing the Levitical priesthood which was superseded by Christ, states: "Every high priest is taken from among men and made their representative before God, to offer gifts and sacrifices for sins." (Heb. 5:1) But what other priests and their sacrifices failed to achieve, Jesus has accomplished "once for all by his sacrifice." (Heb. 9:26) We, his ordained ministers, perpetuate His eternal sacrifice when, obeying Jesus' command at the Last Supper, we "do this" with the bread and wine and so "proclaim the death of the Lord until he comes!" (1 Cor. 11:26)

Although the Letter to the Hebrews does not speak directly of the Church's ministerial priesthood, it identifies an essential condition of fruitful priestly ministry. Referring to the high priest of the Old Covenant, it says: "He is able to deal patiently with erring sinners, for he himself is beset by weakness and so must make sin offerings for himself as well as for the people." (Heb. 5:2-3) Despite our special identity and our unique role as priests of the New Covenant, we remain human, subject to the same weaknesses and shortcomings as all our sisters and brothers. This imposes on us a double imperative.

First, we should approach our ministry with humility. We are not better than others. We are no less in need of forgiveness. Many of those we serve are actually closer to the Lord than we are. Our ministry will be fruitful to the extent that we recognize these truths. We must never lord it over people, never give an impression of moral superiority or increase the burden of guilt which many bear already.

Second, we need to strive for understanding and compassion in all our dealings with others. Surely, this was how Jesus ministered to the people of His day. Consider His great tenderness and compassion toward Mary Magdalene, the woman caught in adultery, the repentant thief on the cross. Ever mindful of our own weakness, we will be better able, in the words of the Letter to the Hebrews, "to deal patiently with erring sinners." In this way even our failings can be made fruitful.

In his priestly role, then, the ordained minister is the source of sacramental contact with Christ. As such, he brings together the human and the divine; he can bring strength out of weakness; he can turn the ridiculous into the sublime.

We Are Shepherds

One of the most beautiful images of Christ is that of shepherd. In chapter 10 of John's gospel Jesus calls Himself the good shepherd and explains what this means. The good shepherd, He says, finds pasture for his sheep; he brings back to the fold those who have strayed; if necessary, he lays down his life for them.

We find this same image at the end of chapter 9 in Matthew's gospel, where Jesus describes what goes on in the shepherd's mind and heart. Jesus had been touring the villages and towns, proclaiming the good news of God's reign to the people and curing them of sickness and disease. Now the crowds lay before Him "prostrate from exhaustion, like sheep without a shepherd." This exhaustion, I believe, refers both to their physical and spiritual condition. The point, in any case, is that the Lord pitied them and did all He could to help them. But He realized that He needed others to assist Him in this task. "The harvest is good," He told His disciples, "but laborers are scarce. Beg the harvest master to send out laborers to gather his harvest." (Matt. 9:35-38)

We priests are among those laborers; we have been sent out by the harvest master. We must be the kind of laborers Jesus wants us to be. Not hirelings indifferent to the people among and with whom they work, but, like Jesus Himself, shepherds who have great concern and affection for the sheep entrusted to them, shepherds eager to do all they can to help the flock, even to the point of giving their own lives.

The image of shepherd supports and enriches the concept of the priest as servant. The Bishops' Committee on Priestly Life and Ministry strongly emphasized this concept in *As One Who Serves*. The priest, the Committee stated, "is to be a servant to the People of God, holding them accountable for what they have been and can be. He serves them by calling forth leadership and coordinating ministries. His is a service which calls the people to remember and to celebrate the presence and power of the Risen Lord. In the fullest sense, he is a servant of the human family."[13]

Our hearts must be moved with pity when we see people who are suffering, whose lives are empty, who are searching vainly for meaning. Through our ministry and our presence, we must do all we can to bring them the riches of the gospel, so that they will come to know the Lord and experience His love and peace in their lives. This is the shepherd's work. This is *our* work as priests who follow in the footsteps of the Good Shepherd and carry on His mission.

A priest — because of the Person he represents and the message he brings — is one whose ministry is expected to bring people joy, consolation, and hope. Admittedly, a priest cannot remove all the pain and frustration which are part of the human condition. But his ministry can help people cope better with trials and sufferings by seeing them in the light of the Transcendent. While we are obliged to do all we can to promote a better life in this world by building a society rooted in justice and love, in the final analysis our earthly accomplishments and their immediate joys and sorrows are transitory. The ultimate fulfillment of all we attempt, the lasting remedy for all we suffer, lie in life eternal.

My personal experience convinces me that what

people actually want and need is usually much less complex and spectacular than we sometimes imagine. People are not looking for religious leaders who can solve all their problems or answer all their questions. Often they know the answers already; or they know their problem has no immediate solution. More than anything else, people look to us who minister to them for our presence as loving, caring, and forgiving people. They want our help in their efforts to handle pain and frustration. They look to us for understanding; they seek a sensitive and consoling response to their hurt feelings; they need the spiritual comfort we can bring through our ministry of word and sacrament. They want someone who will pray with them, whose presence will remind them that, no matter what their difficulties might be, God really loves them and cares for them. They want assurance that God will never abandon them. This is the preferred style of spiritual leadership in our day.

The priest's role as shepherd has another dimension. As we have seen, the ministerial priesthood is Christ's precious, unique gift to His Church, differing from the priesthood of all the baptized not merely in degree but in essence. But Vatican II teaches no less clearly that priestly ministry is exercised *for* and *with* others. The Church is a community of believers in which all members have their own talents, gifts, and responsibilities.

Besides providing those priestly services which only ordination makes possible, we priests therefore have a serious responsibility to help people discover, develop, and use their God-given talents and charisms for the well-being of the Church and society. This is *not* merely a practical necessity imposed by the shortage of priests today. It is a consequence of the rights and obligations of every baptized member of the Church. The Church is poorer whenever any of its members fail to use their gifts. A successful priestly shepherd, therefore, is one who not only *uses his own* charisms, but also knows how to *help others use theirs.*

We find this notion of the priest as an enabler and facilitator in Peter's injunctions to his "fellow-elders," as he called them: "Be examples to the flock, not lording it over those assigned to you, so that when the chief Shepherd appears you will win for yourselves the unfading crown of glory." (1 Pet. 5:3-4)

The image of the priest as shepherd is rich and full of meaning in this regard. It tells us a great deal about his concern for people, his sensitivity to their needs and aspirations, his commitment to provide them with the sustenance and guidance needed to develop their God-given potential so that they can make their specific contribution to the Church. When a priest relates to people in this open and supportive way, he ensures the Church that richness and diversity which God intended and made provision for.

Ministering to people in the manner described here can be difficult. This should not really surprise us. Jesus promised joy and peace, but He also promised the cross — suffering and rejection. We who have committed ourselves to the work of Jesus and seek to model our lives on His must expect the cross.

Ours will be the cross of not seeing clearly at times. The cross of being misunderstood and not being accepted as we are, with all our gifts and limitations. The cross of not fully understanding others. The cross of having to give up some personal idea which once seemed unchangeable, having to get rid of attitudes that used to provide security. The cross of being patient and kind even when, humanly speaking, there seems every reason to fight back, of having compassion for others when precious little has been shown to us. Ours will be the cross of having always to be available, to listen, to learn to start every day as if we were beginning all over again.

But the cross, which is the consequence of sin and death, is only half the story. Fortunately, we know the other half. We rely on God's mercy, on the light of Christ and everlasting life. We console ourselves and others, knowing that "if we have died with him, then we shall live with him. If we hold firm, then we shall reign with him. If we disown him, then he will disown us. We may be unfaithful, but he is always faithful, for he cannot disown his own self." (2 Tim. 2:11-13) Behind the cross is the empty tomb. Let us never forget it.

Personal Qualities for Effective Ministry

BESIDES the personal qualities necessary for fruitful priestly ministry mentioned explicitly or implicitly above, I want to comment on three qualities in particular: faith, fidelity, and the continuing effort to achieve closer union with the Lord.

What I have already said about priestly identity makes sense only within the context of faith. It is in Jesus, whose priesthood we share, that we discover our own specific identity and mission as priests of the New Covenant. But only in faith do we come to know the Lord. Only in faith can we believe and accept the fact that the mystery of Jesus in all its fullness is the basis and foundation of the life and mission of the Church and its priesthood. Jesus Christ is the stable principle and fixed center of the mission that God Himself entrusted to His human creatures.

We shall often not see the fruit of our priestly ministry. This can be especially hard in an age when everyone insists on immediate results. The Letter of James gives us two reasons for patience. Some results take a long time to become visible. More important, the key ingredient of success is always *invisible:* the hidden action of God. "Be patient . . . my brothers," he said, "until the coming of the Lord. See how the farmer awaits the precious yield of the soil. He looks forward to it patiently while the soil receives the winter and the spring rains. You, too, must be patient." (James, 5:7-8)

Continuing to minister to people with undiminished enthusiasm and dedication, while seeing little or no evidence that our efforts have accomplished anything, requires *deep faith.* Only by trusting in the Lord and His saving power can we avoid becoming discouraged and giving up in the face of apathy and the apparent failure of our efforts. We are doing the Lord's work, not our own. Though He chooses to work through us, it is not we who determine whether or when our ministry will succeed. Regardless of how others judge our efforts, they will ultimately be fruitful only if they truly reflect what the Lord expects of us. This conviction will spare us the frustration and despair which can drain our priestly vocation of vitality and hope.

The second requirement of fruitful priestly ministry is *fidelity*. "Men should regard us as servants of Christ and administrators of the mysteries of God. The first requirement of an administrator is that he prove trustworthy." (1 Cor. 4:1-2) This trustworthiness or fidelity is rooted in faith and love. It must be first to the Lord, and then to our sisters and brothers for His sake. In John's gospel Jesus' thrice repeated command to Peter to "feed my lambs . . . tend my sheep" is preceded each time by the question: "Simon, Son of John, do you love me" (John 21:15-17) The questions were wounding to Peter. But they were necessary. Without Peter's threefold pledge of love, the special ministry of service entrusted to him would have lacked a firm basis, one capable of sustaining him in good times and bad.

The presence in our own lives and ministry of this same fidelity — a fidelity grounded in faith and love and drawing inspiration from Christ's fidelity to His Father — gives people encouragement and hope. It assures them that the love, mercy, compassion, and healing of Jesus will always be available to them. It builds up confidence, giving people a sense of the Transcendent and certainty that they will never be alone, never be abandoned, in their earthly pilgrimage.

The fidelity of which I speak demands many things of us. First, it requires that we incarnate in our lives the values which Jesus taught us. As leaders of the Christian community, we must be the first to shape our lives according to His teaching. Otherwise our ministry becomes hypocritical.

Fidelity also demands that we remain open to God's Spirit as He continues to work in and through us until the very end. There is nothing more debilitating, nothing more destructive for us personally and for the people whom we serve, than a refusal to grow, a refusal to be open to the new possibilities presented to us each day. Unless we are open to God's Spirit, a *rigor mortis* sets in which robs our ministry of its creativity and richness.

Finally, fidelity demands that we live up to the specific commitments we make as priests. In his 1979 letter to the priests of the Church, Pope John Paul spoke of the necessity of "keeping one's word to Christ and the Church."[14] Faithfulness to our special commitments as priests, and in particular to our mission, enhances the credibility and effectiveness of our ministry.

Fidelity to the values and personal witness of Jesus, to God's Spirit ever working among us, and to our ecclesial commitments is thus essential if our ministry is to bear fruit as Christ expects. Fidelity of this kind is possible, however, only if we are making a *continuing effort for closer union with the Lord.* Jesus made this clear when, in His last discourse, He told His disciples: "I am the vine, you are the branches. He who lives in me and I in him, will produce abundantly, for apart from me you can do nothing." (John 15:5)

If we preach the gospel in its integrity, if we continue Christ's work which has become a countersign in today's world, we shall encounter misunderstanding, rejection, and persecution. Jesus prepares us for this in advance when He warns: "The reason the world hates you is that you do not belong to the world . . . . Remember what I told you: No slave is greater than his master. They will harry you as they harried me." (John 15:19-20)

We can survive the indifference and the hostility of those who do not want their consciences troubled by Jesus and His teaching *only* by being so closely united with Him that His strength becomes ours. By ourselves we cannot endure very long. But if we unite ourselves with the Lord we shall be able to say with Paul: "I have been crucified with Christ, and the life I live now is not my own; Christ is living in me. I still live my human life, but it is a life of faith in the Son of God, who loved me and gave himself for me." (Gal. 2:19-20)

This close union with Jesus is not just a remote possibility, something for a few specially chosen souls alone. Rather, it is something Jesus is eager to share with everyone of us. This is why He told His apostles: "You are my friends, if you do what I command you. I no longer speak of you as slaves . . . . It was not you who chose me, it was I who chose you, to go forth and bear fruit." (John 15:14-16)

We enter this close union with Jesus by totally abandoning ourselves to Him, by placing ourselves in His hands so that we can be instruments mediating His love and mercy, and by constantly nourishing our union with Him through prayer.

The Prayer Life of the Priest

PRAYER is a marvelous reality which can truly transform our lives. Its ultimate goal, of course, is to bring us into closer union with Jesus. In doing this, however, it also helps us come to a better knowledge of ourselves and relate in a more loving, intimate way to others.

Renewed interest in spirituality and prayer is much in evidence today. Despite material and secular pressures, people are praying. We see this in the popularity of such phenomena as the charismatic renewal and oriental mysticism. To cite only one small example from my personal experience, in the fall of 1978 I was invited to celebrate Mass for new students and their parents at the University of Dayton. Previously the service had always been held in the small university chapel, with seldom more than several hundred in attendance. On this occasion — simply because of the interest of the students themselves — it took place in the arena, with nearly 2,000 present.

This renewed interest in prayer is a reaffirmation of a tradition as old as the Church itself. Jesus was a man of prayer. The gospels tell us He prayed before all the important events in His life. Before beginning His public ministry, He went into the desert to fast and pray for forty days. And what intense prayer He experienced in the Garden of Gethsemane the night before making the supreme gift of Himself to His Father on our behalf! St. Paul, in his letters, constantly focused on his need for prayer and the need of others. "Never cease praying," he told the Thessalonians, "render constant thanks, such is God's will for you in Christ Jesus." (1 Thess. 5:16)

To be a follower of Christ, then, one must be a person of prayer. But it is important to know what prayer really involves. What kind of prayer were Jesus and the apostles talking about? What effect should prayer have on people, especially on us who are priests? Authentic prayer will have a tremendous effect in our lives. Contrary to what some have intimated, in no way should prayer insulate us from the real world. In no way should it become a crutch on which we lean to avoid facing up realistically to life. Quite the contrary. Authentic prayer — that is, prayer which brings us into an intimate, loving union with God — will deeply affect how we perceive and deal with *ourselves* and with *others*. I hope my reflections, which flow from my own spiritual journey, will help and encourage you to persevere in yours. Even if I do not shed much light on the dark areas you have encountered, it may be that simply knowing you are not alone will encourage you to continue.

Prayer as Discovery of Self

Spiritual writers tell us there are many kinds of prayer. The four classical forms are vocal (that is, prayer expressed in words, either a fixed formula or one's own words), meditative, affective, and contemplative. In the final analysis, however, each must pray in the way that best lifts his or her mind and heart to the Lord. Regardless of the particular method we use or the facility we may have developed, prayer, if it is genuine, must move us to a greater knowledge of ourselves. St. Teresa of Avila holds that one cannot grow closer to God without constantly growing in self-knowledge.[15] Precisely for this reason, real growth in prayer involves a movement toward greater simplicity, that is, fewer words and thoughts. Both John of the Cross and Teresa say our own words and thoughts may lead us in the wrong direction; they may distract us from what God wants to show us about ourselves.

I hasten to add that prayer is not simply a process of introspection and self-analysis. But it is also true that God cannot help us if we are unwilling to present ourselves to Him as we really are. The well-known Orthodox prelate Archbishop Anthony Bloom states: "Throughout the day we are a succession of social personalities, sometimes unrecognizable . . . even to ourselves. And when the time comes to pray and we want to present ourselves to God, we often feel lost because we do not know which of these social personalities is the true human person, and we have no sense of our own true identity . . . . God can save only the true person; He cannot save the imaginary person."[16]

If we are honest, we must admit that much of our time is spent pretending. But when we turn to God in prayer, we must present our real selves, candidly acknowledging our strengths and weaknesses and our total dependence on Him. To experience true conversion, we must first come to grips with our innermost selves, those selves which exist independently of external circumstances and pressures.

Let us consider some practical implications of self-knowledge. Basically, to know oneself in prayer is to know one's motives. What motivates my life, my decisions, my actions, my ministry? Prayer should lead to honesty. For example, is one's motivation the need for acceptance or recognition? Is it competition, fear, insecurity, resentment? Honesty often leads to the conclusion that, although the motivation is not all "bad," it is quite imperfect. As such, it can lead us away from Jesus and the way of life He has given us.

In his letter to the Galatians, Paul describes certain forms of conduct arising from motivations which are of the Spirit, along with forms of conduct arising from promptings and inclinations which are not. His description gives a good yardstick for making a judgment about ourselves. "It is obvious," he said, "what proceeds from the flesh: lewd conduct, impurity, licentiousness, idolatry, sorcery, hostilities, bickering, jealousy, outbursts of rage, selfish rivalries, dissension, factions, envy, drunkenness, orgies, and the like . . . . In contrast, the fruit of the spirit is love, joy, peace, patient endurance, kindness, generosity, faith, mildness, and chastity . . . since we live by the spirit let us follow the spirit's lead. Let us never be boastful, or challenging, or jealous toward one another." (Gal. 5:19-26)

As we move closer to God, everything within us which is not of God will be disclosed. If, on the other hand, we fail to recognize motivations or movements within us which are not of God, if we do not recognize the evil in us, that failure itself becomes an obstacle to closer union with the Lord. Often, of course, we are not fully conscious of what motivates us. It is very easy to fool ourselves. This is why we need a spiritual director who, along with other vital positive assistance rendered to us on our spiritual journey, can help us make sure that we are objective and correct in judging what is going on inside us.

Another important point: Discovering our true selves can be a very painful experience. At first we tend to rebel when we confront our ugly side. This pain, however, is to be expected. We have been warned to expect the cross in our lives, and sometimes the cross comes not from outside us but from within. Did not Jesus say: "If a man wishes to come after me, he must deny his very self, take up his cross, and begin to follow in my footsteps"? (Matt. 16:24) In his Letter to the Colossians, Paul goes a step further, saying that our suffering completes the process of purification required for our redemption: "In my own flesh I fill up what is lacking in the sufferings of Christ for the sake of his body, the Church." (Col. 1:24) The suffering entailed in humbly acknowledging our own weakness and imperfection can itself be redemptive. Spiritual satisfaction is certainly not the necessary and exclusive sign that God loves us and is pleased with us. On the contrary, spiritual writers tell us that even for those who have committed themselves to prayer over long periods of time, the prevailing experience is not satisfaction, but "dryness." This certainly has been my experience. To think that because we have put in our "time" we have a right to expect a "return" in the form of satisfaction is spiritual selfishness. Authentic prayer is concerned not so much with getting as with giving.

Despite the dryness, however, if we are men of faith and fidelity, we will continue to feel a certain restlessness or hunger calling us to communion with the Lord. For God never abandons us. He is always present, calling us to Himself. As Father John Shea tells us in *Stories of God:* "God is a passionate presence to all human life, never deserting it . . . . The love of God demands he be wherever his creation is."[17] Hunger for communion with the Lord even in the midst of dryness is actually the *gift* by which God calls us to Himself.[18]

This gift implants within us the desire to grow spiritually, to abandon ourselves completely to the Lord, to risk encountering the Lord in prayer. And "risk" it is. For, as Archbishop Bloom remarks, the encounter with God (and our fellow human beings) in prayer is "dangerous." "It is not without reason," he says, "that the eastern tradition of Zen calls the place where we find him whom we seek the tiger's lair. Seeking God is an act of boldness, unless it is an act of complete humility. Encountering God is always a crisis."[19] The reason is simple: God's demands can be overpowering; humanly speaking, they can be embarrassing, even devastating! We may find ourselves called to make a radical and even painful response. Yet

God calls us to trust enough in His love for us and His power within us to be willing to risk knowing ourselves and encountering Him.

Prayer as Discovery of Others

Prayer therefore brings us closer to God only if it helps us discover ourselves at the same time. However painful it may be, we must strive to present our true selves to the Lord so that He will have a real person, not an imaginary one, to love and comfort. But prayer also involves another dimension. As it brings us closer to God, it also helps us to discover others. It involves a movement toward greater intimacy with others: with God first, of course, but also and in a particular way with other men and women.

The testimony of Scripture supports this view. Jesus made it very clear that love of God cannot be separated from love of neighbor. "This is the first [of all the commandments]," He said, " 'Hear, O Israel! The Lord our God is Lord alone! Therefore, you shall love the Lord your God with all your heart, with all your soul, with all your mind, and with all your strength.' This is the second, 'you shall love your neighbor as yourself.' " (Mark, 12:29-31)

The basis for this inseparable link between love of God and love of neighbor is the Incarnation. The Father so loved us that He sent His Son to redeem us. Jesus became flesh and lived among us. The Incarnation establishes such a close and intimate relationship — between us and God, and also among us human beings — that we can now call ourselves sons and daughters of the Father and brothers and sisters of.and in the Lord. If we want to follow the Lord, we must also love all those whom He loves. There is no other way.

We often experience tension between love of God and love of others. In His great parable of the last judgment Jesus shows that for God the two are inseparable. "Then the just will ask him: 'Lord, when did we see you hungry and feed you or see you thirsty and give you drink? When did we welcome you away from home and clothe you in your nakedness? When did we visit you when you were ill or in prison?' The king will answer them: 'I assure you, as often as you did it for one of my least brothers, you did it for me.' " (Matt. 25:37-40)

The German theologian Walter Kasper says: "The solidarity of God with men manifested and realized in Jesus Christ establishes a new solidarity among men. The Christian idea of representation then assigns to Christians and to the churches the world as the place of their service and binds them to cooperate in a new order of peace in freedom sustained by the idea of solidarity."[20]

Our faith and everything that flows from it — including our prayer — must be understood in its incarnational perspective. That includes not only our new relationship, as a redeemed people, to God but also our new relationship to all of God's children. Part of this relationship is the God-given capacity to love others.

Any consideration of love inevitably touches the area of sexuality. Too often today we identify human sexuality only with its genital aspect. In the past, the words "human sexuality" were usually taken as a synonym for genital pleasure. Since this kind of pleasure was something we priests chose to forego in virtue of our celibate commitment, there was a tendency to ignore, if not deny, our sexuality. As a result, there were many who did not understand its power and its capacity for good even (and perhaps especially) in a celibate. Often, when the power of their sexuality manifested itself, they did not know how to deal with it.

Genital pleasure is certainly a dimension of sexuality, but sexuality itself is a much broader concept. Human sexuality is part of our God-given natural power or capacity for relating to others in a loving, caring way. From it flow the qualities of sensitivity, warmth, openness, and mutual respect in interpersonal relationships. To deny or altogether repress these qualities thus inevitably lessens one's ability to relate to others and truly love them. Such denial or repression can warp our personality and turn us into frightened, threatened, or bitter men.

If on the other hand we are truly alive with God's love within us, this will be reflected in our ability to love others, to be present to them in a caring way. The intimacy of which I speak is not primarily genital, although love obviously can and should be expressed in this way by two persons joined together in the covenant of marriage. For all people, married or single, this intimacy means at least two things.

First, it means willingness to disclose oneself to others, to become somewhat vulnerable with them by being honest about oneself. For many this is difficult. They think that revealing their weaknesses or needs makes them appear weak. And pride or fear blocks any admission of weakness. So they hold things inside, thus allowing pressures to build until, in some cases, they can no longer cope successfully with them.

The Lord has given us a wonderful way of dealing with such pressures in the Sacrament of Reconciliation. Even humanly speaking, people need the opportunity to open up, to get things out of their system. They need a way of coming to grips with their inner selves. They need to hear the words: "I forgive you." This is not to suggest that the Sacrament is primarily a form of therapy. Its operation and benefits are essentially spiritual. But that in no way excludes the wonderful natural benefits which it also confers.

Admittedly, the forum of the confessional is sacred and limited. We may choose not to reveal ourselves even to close friends in the same way we open up to our confessor. But, there are many matters outside the realm of the confessional which cause confusion, anxiety, depression, and other negative feelings and which we could and should share with those who are close to us. More often than not, we will find that our friends experience the same difficulties. That discovery itself establishes a bond of solidarity and understanding which can be mutually beneficial.

Second, intimacy involves willingness to let others become a part of, and an influence on, my life. Then my life and my decisions are not simply my own. I accept some degree of responsibility for those I allow to love me, to care for me, to help me. Willingness to assume responsibility for others is often lacking today. We have all read accounts of people who have been injured, even killed, because bystanders did not want to "get involved." Such cases happily are rare. More often, unwillingness to "get involved" manifests itself in failure to say a kind word, to extend a helping hand when needed, to show some tangible sign of understanding and concern, even when the other person is a friend or associate.

Intimacy, as I have described it, obviously involves the risk of self-sacrifice. However, this should not really surprise us. As we have seen, any intimate encounter with God, with a fellow human being, or with oneself is downright dangerous, in the sense that it can demand radical changes on our part. It can shake us from our lethargy. It requires that we make our peace with God, our neighbor, and even ourselves. It taks a considerable amount of self-discipline to be able to reach out to others so that one can relate to them in a way that is both consistent with one's state in life and conducive to their well-being and growth. There is the risk, of course, of being rejected or feeling foolish, but the risk is worth the advantages which stem from authentic Christian intimacy.

Jesus is Himself the prime model for this intimacy. The gospels show that He had close relationships with many men and women. He often risked His reputation and even His life for those He loved. Eventually, He gave His life so that He could enter into the ultimate intimacy with us, the intimacy of the redemption which reestablished us in God's love and friendship. Paul is another model. He, too, had close relationships with men and women. This is evident in his many letters. Consider, for example, the many people he singled out for special greetings in his Letter to the Romans: "Give my greetings to Prisca and Aquila; they were my fellow workers in the service of Christ Jesus and even risked their lives for the sake of mine . . . Greetings to my beloved Epaenetus; he is the first offering that Asia made to Christ. My greetings to Mary, who has worked hard for you . . . Greetings to Ampliatus, who is dear to me in the Lord; to Urbanus, our fellow worker in the service of Christ; and to my beloved Stachys . . . " (Rom. 16:3-8)

Intimacy is important for fruitful priestly ministry. Obviously, I am not speaking of rash behavior, of gratuitous self-testing and risk-taking. The intimacy of which I speak has a kind of profundity, an almost sacred character. Indeed, I believe a capacity for intimacy, as I have described it, is essential to ministry. Any real inability to be intimate, to be honest and open with others, will limit one's effectiveness in ministry.

How many of our difficulties in ministry are difficulties in relationships (pastor-associate, priest-people, priest-staff, etc.)? Many priests are less effective than they could be, and suffer as a result, because they cannot communicate. They insist on "going it alone," on "stonewalling," when an honest, open discussion of issues or feelings would go a long way toward resolving difficulties. We all know it is not always easy to be open. It is not always easy for me. And I have found, too, that others have difficulty being open with me because they see the bishop as primarily an authority figure. I am convinced that the authority we most need today — and the only kind of authority which is respected and accepted — is the authority of wisdom and, above all, the authority of compassionate love. I need your understanding and support to develop both. To this end I also need your prayers.

Let me relate everything I have been saying about sexuality and intimacy to the life of celibacy to which we committed ourselves when we were ordained. Father Henri Nouwen thinks the best definition of celibacy is that of Thomas Aquinas, who calls celibacy an "emptiness for God" (*vacare Deo*). "To be celibate means to be empty for God, to be free and open for his presence, to be available for his service." Nouwen maintains that this is "an essential part of all forms of Christian life: marriage, friendship, single life, and community life."[21] In every life there must be an inner sanctum reserved for God alone.

"Celibates," Nouwen writes, "live out the holy emptiness in their lives by not marrying, by not trying to wield as much influence as possible, and by not filling their lives with events, people or creations for which they will be remembered. They hope that by their empty lives God will be recognized as the source of all human thoughts and actions. Especially by not marrying and by abstaining from the most intimate expression of human love, the celibate becomes a living sign of the limits of interpersonal relationships and the centrality of the inner sanctum that no human being may violate."[22]

Celibacy is a topic about which there has been much discussion and controversy in recent years. It is important that we understand how celibacy is related to our priesthood. The Church presents celibacy to us as a reality which has far more meaning and richness than a mere law or discipline. It is a "qualification" which enhances the effectiveness of our witness to the gospel and the fruitfulness of our ministry. It is truly an offering — a sacrifice — publicly given for the sake of the kingdom of heaven. Indeed, it transcends the natural order and cannot be maintained without God's grace.

The 1971 Synod, in its document on the ministerial priesthood, put it this way: The candidate for the priesthood "must understand this form of life not as something imposed from without, but rather as an expression of his own free giving, which, in turn, is accepted and ratified by the Church in the person of the Bishop."[23] I firmly believe and accept what the Church teaches about the value of celibacy and its relationship to priesthood.

I know, however, that the life of celibacy, in the practical order, is not the same for all of us. Some find it rather easy to live, while others find it a constant challenge. This is due in part to difference of personality, temperament, and circumstance. But it is also due to another reality that we must frankly admit. Celibacy is perceived and accepted by some in the way the Church sees it: a genuine charism, a gift of the Spirit. It flows from a personal spiritual call to the celibate life. Other priests, however, do not perceive celibacy in this way. They are celibate because of their generous and selfless response to what they consider simply a discipline of the Church rather than a personal charism which is inherent in their call to the priesthood as it is mediated and affirmed by the Church.

Whatever your perception, I urge you not to see celibacy as a negative reality. It is intimately connected with our mission as priests and with the quality and dynamism of our ministry. It is a sign of our total dedication to the Lord and also a means of freeing ourselves so that we may commit ourselves more fully to the service of God and the human family. Moreover, we believe that God gives us the grace needed to live the life of celibacy. Unless we understand and accept celibacy in this way, our ministry will be impeded. Celibacy is not meant to turn us into unloving, insensitive bachelors. Rather, celibacy — correctly understood, truly cherished, and lived with integrity — can help intensify our love for the Lord and for the people we serve.

Since celibacy involves a commitment to accept and integrate the gift of sexuality in a special way, it reflects not a denial of the human need for intimacy but a decision to live out intimacy in a particular way. Growth in the life of celibacy means growing in the capacity to love others without seeking the exclusivity of marriage. The mature and prayerful celibate priest is one whose "emptiness" is filled up with love of God and God's people.

I began by saying that if prayer is authentic, it will lead to a discovery both of ourselves and of others. It involves a movement toward greater knowledge of self and greater intimacy with others. We cannot be truly in love with the Lord, we cannot really be in communion with Him through prayer, without its having a profound effect on our personal growth and our relationships with others. Growth in prayer, while an interior phenomenon, is reflected in how we live. Especially is it reflected in the visible manifestation of our love for others.

Paul, in his letter to the Corinthians, described that manifestation in this way: "Love is patient; love is kind. Love is not jealous, it does not put on airs, it is not snobbish. Love is never rude, it is not self-seeking, it is not prone to anger; neither does it brood over injuries. Love does not rejoice in what is wrong but rejoices with the truth. There is no limit to love's forbearance, to its trust, its hope, its power to endure. Love never fails . . . ." (1 Cor. 13:4-8)

Can you imagine how life in this local church would change if everyone, especially you and I, began relating to others in this way? Our parishes and institutions, our rectories and offices, above all our lives and ministries would all give, for the entire world, a credible and compelling witness to Christ's lordship.

Afterword

MY dear brothers in Christ! Before concluding, I want to share some deeply personal thoughts and convictions.

I wish first to tell you of God's great goodness to me. I have experienced doubts, temptations, anxieties, difficulties of every kind. I am sure you have also. In reflecting on my shortcomings and sinfulness, I have been discouraged and even depressed. I have often dealt with people who did not understand me or questioned my motives or even rejected my ministry. This has caused me to feel disillusioned, rejected, even angry. It is part of the human condition to experience these feelings. Not even Jesus was spared all of them.

Yet through it all, God has been at my side. His goodness to me has been overwhelming. When I did not know which way to turn, He gave me direction. When I did not measure up to His expectations, He forgave me — over and over again. He has given me the strength and motivation needed to continue the struggle. He has always been present to wipe away the tears of discouragement and loneliness. So often all I could produce were the proverbial crooked lines, yet somehow He always managed to write straight with them.

Another person who has played an important role in my life is Mary. The late Pope Paul VI said Mary, as the perfect Christian, was a model for all Christians.[24] In a very special way, however, she is a model and source of inspiration and strength for priests. Her greatness rests in her intense faith, which prompted her to accept God's will joyfully and without hesitation. Her example and intercession have been a precious gift to me.

I make Mary's song of praise my own today, as I recall God's goodness to me during the many years I have been privileged to serve as a priest and bishop: "My soul proclaims the greatness of the Lord, my spirit rejoices in God my Savior, for he has looked with favor on his lowly servant." (Luke 1:46-48)

What have been the happiest times of my priestly

ministry? I can answer without hesitation: the times when I have been nearest to the people — when I could bring them the beauty and richness of Christ's word and the consolation and healing power of His sacraments; when I could share their joys and sorrows; when, through my presence, I could give them assurance that — notwithstanding all their shortcomings and failures — they were important in the Lord's eyes.

Contemporary society has its own standards for judging a person's success. But nothing of what the world calls success can begin to compare with the grace-filled experiences I have had in ministering to people. The satisfaction that comes from such ministry is our greatest reward. It is far better than prominence, official position, or the fleeting applause of crowds.

One final word. The Church in which you and I minister today is quite different from the Church in which many of us were ordained. Those of you who are younger may not fully appreciate what has occurred in the past fifteen or twenty years. I can assure you that a tremendous change has taken place, not in the basic nature of the Church and its priesthood, but in our ministerial style and our vision of how we should relate to a fast-changing world.

It has not always been easy to adapt. There have been times when I was perplexed, even troubled. But despite the puzzlement caused by changes which could not possibly have been imagined on the day of my priestly ordination — when everything seemed so tranquil and settled — I thank God for it all. The turmoil of these years has been the birth pangs of a new age and a renewed Church. Far from weakening my faith, the events of the past few years have strengthened it. My union with the Lord has become more intimate and decisive.

For all this I express gratitude to God and to you, my brothers, who have supported and encouraged me. May the Lord bless us as, together, we rededicate ourselves to what, after almost three decades, I am more than ever convinced is the greatest service in the world.

Your brother in Christ,

+Joseph L. Bernardin

Footnotes

1. *Dogmatic Constitution on the Church,* II Vatican Council, 1964, par. 10

2. Jaroslav Pelikan, *The Riddle of Roman Catholicism,* Abington Press, p. 22

3. *Dogmatic Constitution on the Church,* par. 10

4. Bishops' Committee on Priestly Life and Ministry, *As One Who Serves,* USCC Publications Office, 1977, p. 21

5. Pope John Paul II, "Address to the Roman Clergy," *Catholic Mind,* LXXVII, March, 1979, par. 2

6. *The Roman Pontifical,* 1978, pp. 207-208

7. *Letter of the Supreme Pontiff John Paul II to All Priests of the Church on the Occasion of Holy Thursday 1979,* Vatican City, Vatican Polyglot Press, 1979, par. 10

8. Pope Paul VI, *On Evangelization in the Modern World,* USCC Publications Office, 1976, par. 76

9. *Letter of the Supreme Pontiff Pope John Paul II to All the Bishops of the Church on the Mystery and Worship of the Holy Eucharist,* Vatican City, Vatican Polyglot Press, 1980, par. 2

10. *Ibid.,* par. 5

11. *Ibid.,* par. 6

12. *The Constitution on the Sacred Liturgy,* II Vatican Council, 1963, par. 10

13. Bishops' Committee on Priestly Life and Ministry, *Ibid.,* p. 54

14. *Letter to All Priests,* par. 9

15. Cf. St. Teresa of Avila, *The Interior Castle,* Paulist Press, 1979, Sec. 1, chap. 2

16. Anthony Bloom and Georges Lefebvre, *Courage to Pray,* Paulist Press, 1973, p. 18

17. John Shea, *Stories of God,* Thomas More Press, 1978, p. 151

18. Cf. Thomas H. Green, S. J., *When the Well Runs Dry,* Ave Maria Press, 1979, chap. 3

19. Anthony Bloom and Georges Lefebvre, *ibid.*, p. 15

20. Walter Kasper, *Jesus the Christ*, Paulist Press, 1977, p. 225

21. Henri J. M. Nouwen, *Clowning in Rome*, Image Books, 1979, p. 45

22. Henri J. M. Nouwen, *ibid.*, pp. 48-49

23. *The Ministerial Priesthood*, 1971 Synod of Bishops, USCC Publications Office, 1972, Part Two, Sec. I, No. 4.

24. Cf. Pope Paul VI, *Marialis Cultus*, *L'Osservatore Romano*, April 4, 1974, par. 34-37

Illustrations

Cover illustration and page vi are details from *Christ Preaching*, etching and drypoint ca. 1612, by Rembrandt Harmensz van Rijn. Cincinnati Art Museum, bequest of Herbert Greer French.

Illustration on page 8 from *Christ at Emmaus: The Larger Plate*, etching, 1654, by Rembrandt Harmensz van Rijn. Cincinnati Art Museum, gift of Herbert Greer French.

Illustration on page 24 from *Raising of Lazarus: The Smaller Plate*, etching, 1642, by Rembrandt Harmensz van Rijn. Cincinnati Art Museum, gift of Herbert Greer French.

Illustration on page 32 from *Christ on the Mount of Olives*, etching, 1515, by Albrecht Durer. Cincinnati Art Museum, gift of Herbert Greer French.